IF PREHISTORIC BEASTS WERE HERE TODAY

EARTH'S GIANTS

Thanks to the creative team:

Senior Editor: Alice Peebles
Consultant: Neil Clark
Fact checking: Kate Mitchell
Design: www.collaborate.agency

First published in Great Britain in 2016
by Hungry Tomato Ltd
PO Box 181
Edenbridge
Kent, TN8 9DP

A CIP catalogue record for this book is
available from the British Library.

ISBN 978-1-910684-74-0

Printed and bound in China

Discover more at
www.hungrytomato.com

IF PREHISTORIC BEASTS WERE HERE TODAY

EARTH'S GIANTS

by Matthew Rake
Illustrated by Simon Mendez

HUNGRY
TOMATO™

WARNING! These extinct beasts are not alive today. But just imagine if they were...

CONTENTS

THE BIG, THE BAD AND THE UGLY

We all know the dinosaurs reached ginormous proportions. But they weren't the only colossal creatures to roam the world before humans. Read on to discover some of the biggest, baddest and ugliest animals ever to inhabit the planet.

Opabinia

So how did these creatures evolve? Well, all life started in the sea – and around 545 million years ago, many different animals began to appear. Some of them were truly weird. Take *Opabinia* (left). It had five mushroom-shaped eyes, 15 body segments, and a grasping claw at the end of a long, hose-like arm. It used this to feed itself, rather like the elephant uses its trunk.

Out of the water, things got just as bizarre. About 300 million years ago, huge dragonflies took to the air. They had wingspans stretching to 65 cm (26 in) – the same size as some of today's birds of prey. And below them, massive millipedes – up to 2.3 m (7 ft 6 in) long – marched across the land. It sounds like science fiction, but these creatures really existed.

The first dinosaurs evolved about 240–230 million years ago, but they didn't rule the world straightaway. Most, like *Compsognathus* (left), were only the size of turkeys. But they were fast, and preyed on tiny reptiles and mammals that scampered around the forests. Over 40 million years or so, dinosaurs became massive for various reasons, including a super-abundance of food.

Compsognathus with prey

Mammals started evolving at the same time as dinosaurs. For about 160 million years, however, most mammals were shrew-sized – any larger and they would have been gobbled up by hungry carnivorous dinosaurs.

After the dinosaurs died out, mammals, such as the giant sloth *Megatherium* (below), grew to enormous proportions. You might think today's gorillas, elephants, camels and rhinos are big – but they are all dwarfed by their prehistoric ancestors. And even they looked small compared to the biggest land mammal of all time – *Paraceratherium* (left).

Here we bring these animals back to life, and show you what they would look like in today's world. So read on to witness an invasion from a prehistoric world...

Paraceratherium

...and get ready for some bizarre and scary encounters between humans (or animals) and mighty beasts.

Megatherium

HEAD-BUTTING BEAST

MOSCHOPS

These days, there are people who earn money by walking dogs. It sounds like a nice job, with lots of fresh air and exercise. But surely this dog walker should be getting paid extra? After all, look at that beast she's having to deal with. It's a *Moschops*, a massive mammal-like reptile that lived before the age of the dinosaurs. And, with a big, barrel-shaped body on top of those short legs, it doesn't look as if it wants to go anywhere fast.

Trying to encourage it to get a move on might not be the wisest move. *Moschops'* skull was up to 10 cm (4 in) thick – that's the width of a brick! It used it to head-butt rival *Moschops*, and some scientists even think they got on their hind legs to fight, like sumo wrestlers. So if this *Moschops* wants go at its own pace, this dog walker should let it!

MOSCHOPS

PRONOUNCED
MOSS-chops

LIVED
Forests of
South Africa,
267–260 million
years ago

LENGTH
About 2.7 m (9 ft)

WEIGHT
About 914 kg (2,000 lb)

TV STAR

In the 1980s, a *Moschops* was the star of an animated TV series of that name. The show also featured his friend Ally, an *Allosaurus*, grandfather *Diplodocus* and Uncle Rex (yes, a *T. rex*). It wasn't exactly accurate. All the animals actually lived millions and millions of years apart!

HORNED HORROR

ESTEMMENOSUCHUS

So what on Earth is this crazy-looking creature? Is it a croc? A hippo? A combination of the two? No, it's an *Estemmenosuchus*. And it's not some sort of dinosaur either – this mammal-like reptile lived about 25 million years before the first dinosaurs came along.

Don't worry – if *Estemmenosuchus* looks like a confusing creature to you, it is for scientists, too. They can't work out whether it was a carnivore (meat-eater) or a herbivore (plant-eater). Its sharp canine and incisor teeth look as if they were made for ripping into flesh. But its big body seems made for digesting plant matter. And its short, widely set front legs are perfect for lowering its head to the ground to graze on plants. Maybe it's an omnivore, so it ate both meat and plants.

Whatever the answer, it doesn't look as if it will back down in this stand-off with a lion. It might not be the speediest of animals, but with its huge horns and beefy body it can probably look after itself. Its skull alone, at 65 cm (26 in), is twice the length of the lion's. The king of the jungle might just have a rival for its crown.

ESTEMMENOSUCHUS
PRONOUNCED
Ess-tim-en-oh-SUE-kuss
LIVED
Russia, about 267 million years ago
LENGTH
Up to 4.5 m (15 ft)
WEIGHT
About 450 kg (990 lb)

HEY, GOOD-LOOKIN'

The horns of *Estemmenosuchus* grew upwards and outwards from the skull bones, and were probably designed for attracting mates, just as a peacock's feathers attract peahens.

BIG BEAST IN THE BIG APPLE

PARACERATHERIUM

OK, what's the world's largest land mammal? An elephant? That's right if we are talking about today's world. But the largest land mammal of all time was *Paraceratherium*. It weighed four times more than an African elephant and was twice as tall. And it looks like it's just come back from the dead!

Don't worry, no one's directly in danger here. *Paraceratherium* is a herbivore and it's probably looking for a park with a few trees to snack on. The pedestrians just need to make sure they don't get caught under its feet, because it doesn't look like the nimblest of creatures. For the best (and safest) view, they probably should go inside a building – preferably three flights up for a great face-to-face encounter!

Paraceratherium is closely related to the rhino, but it lived like a giraffe, using its great height to feed on the tasty leaves out of reach of other animals. Scientists think it used its big incisor teeth to hold the branches and its big muscular lips to rip off the leaves.

PARACERATHERIUM

PRONOUNCED
Para-sera-THEE-rium

LIVED
Asia, 34–23 million
years ago

HEIGHT
5 m (16 ft), at the shoulder

LENGTH
8 m (26 ft)

WEIGHT
15–20 tonnes
(16.5–22 US tons)

HEAVIEST MAMMAL

Paraceratherium might be the heaviest ever land mammal, but it can't compare with the blue whale, the heaviest mammal of all. At about 180 tonnes (200 US tons), the blue whale is 10 times heavier – and it is still around today, despite being hunted almost to extinction in the 20th century.

TITANIC TURTLE
STUPENDEMYS

You'd probably think that the massive turtle *Stupendemys* would have been safe from predators 10 million years ago, when it lived in the waters of what became the River Amazon. Surely no other animal would have taken on this Titan with its supersize, shield-like shell. But *Stupendemys* lived at the same time as some of the biggest crocs ever to lurk in Earth's watery places. *Purusaurus*, for instance, could grow to a massive 13 m (42 ft) long, weighed around 8.5 tonnes (9 US tons), and probably would have made short work of *Stupendemys*.

However, *Stupendemys* doesn't have much to worry about here in the Everglades of Florida, USA. It can take a relaxing dip in the swamp waters safe in the knowledge that even the largest alligators, at 4 m (13 ft), are not going make much impression on that shell.

STUPENDEMYS
PRONOUNCED
Stoo-PEND-ee-miss
LIVED
Northern South America, 10–5 million years ago
SHELL LENGTH
About 3 x 2 m
(10 x 6 ft 6 in)
WEIGHT
About 1.5 tonnes
(1.6 US tons)

UNDERWATER EATER

Stupendemys wasn't the only giant turtle to prowl around the Amazon in days gone by. *Carbonemys* lived about 50 million years earlier, its shell was about 1.7 m (5 ft 6 in) long, and it had powerful jaws capable of eating small crocs.

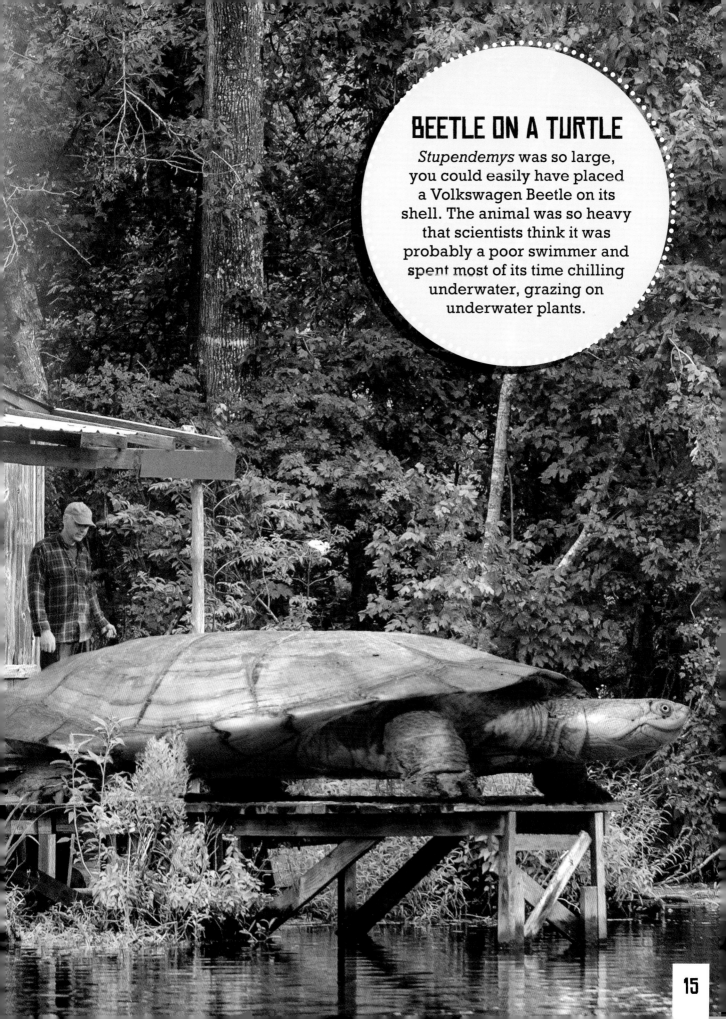

BEETLE ON A TURTLE

Stupendemys was so large, you could easily have placed a Volkswagen Beetle on its shell. The animal was so heavy that scientists think it was probably a poor swimmer and spent most of its time chilling underwater, grazing on underwater plants.

MONKEY BUSINESS

GIGANTOPITHECUS

Who is this unexpected visitor to the Great Wall of China? Meet *Gigantopithecus*, the biggest ape ever to walk the Earth. It's twice the height of a gorilla and three times its weight – but, even so, it's not a danger to the sightseers. By studying its teeth and jaws, scientists have discovered that *Gigantopithecus* liked a diet of fruit, nuts and shoots. Some scientists think it might have gobbled up the occasional small mammal or lizard, but only as a side dish.

Although *Gigantopithecus* might look like a gorilla, its closest living relative is actually the orangutan. Like the orangutan, it lived in forests – but it found it harder and harder to find food when, around 100,000 years ago, the climate began to get cooler and forests started shrinking. And of course, unlike the orangutan, it would have missed out on all the fruit growing in the treetops. It might be able to climb the Great Wall of China, but it was far too heavy to climb trees!

GIGANTOPITHECUS

PRONOUNCED
Jye-GAN-toe-PITH-eh-kuss

LIVED
China, India, Vietnam and Nepal, 9 million–100,000 years ago

LENGTH
3 m (10 ft)

WEIGHT
540 kg (1,190 lb)

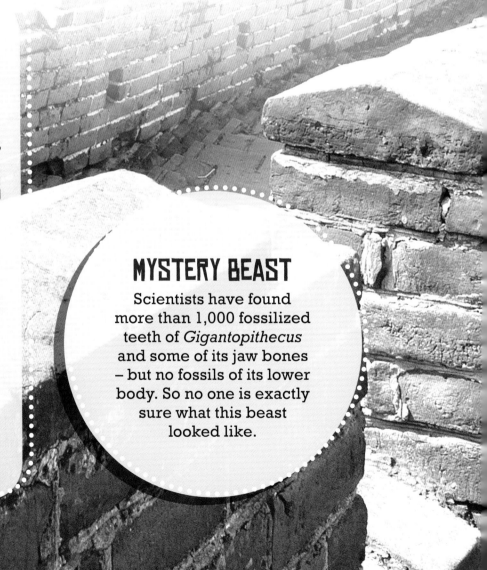

MYSTERY BEAST
Scientists have found more than 1,000 fossilized teeth of *Gigantopithecus* and some of its jaw bones – but no fossils of its lower body. So no one is exactly sure what this beast looked like.

RUNAWAY RHINO
ELASMOTHERIUM

Every July, charging bulls, led by human runners, are let loose on the streets of Pamplona in Spain. And yes, they cause complete havoc. Running at an average speed of 24 km/h (15 mph), the bulls usually injure between 50 and 100 people. Those who slip or are pushed over are the lucky ones – you just want to avoid being gored on those horns!

This year, things have got a whole lot more dangerous because look what has joined the fun: an *Elasmotherium*. That's a giant rhino to you and me. These creatures were the size of elephants – about 4 tonnes (4.4 US tons) of solid flesh, bone and muscle. They were covered in hair and scientists think they galloped like horses. What's more, while bulls' horns seem dangerous, check out *Elasmotherium*'s. Now the bulls seem in as much danger as the runners...

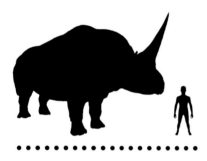

ELASMOTHERIUM
PRONOUNCED
Eh-laz-moe-THEE-ree-um

LIVED
Plains of Asia and
Eastern Europe,
2 million–30,000 years
ago

LENGTH
6 m (20 ft)

WEIGHT
3-4 tonnes
(3.3-4.4 US tons)

HEIGHT
2 m (6 ft 6 in)

MISSING HORNS

Elasmotherium's horn was made from keratin – the same substance that makes up human hair and fingernails. Unfortunately, this doesn't fossilize well, so nobody knows the exact length of the horn. But scientists think it was about 1.75 m (5 ft 9 in) long.

LIVED WITH HUMANS

In 2016, new research on a piece of *Elasmotherium* skull found in Kazakhstan showed that the animal lived until about 30,000 years ago. Previously scientists thought it had died out 350,000 years ago. This means the creature lived at the same time as humans.

MAGNIFICENT MARSUPIAL

DIPROTODON

Looks like we have an extra player for the volleyball match. Not sure that this pigeon-toed creature is going to be the best team-mate, though. It doesn't look like it can make the sharpest moves, or has the fastest reactions.

So who – or what – is this new player? It's a *Diprotodon* and it lived in Australia until 40,000 years ago. Like Australia's kangaroo and koala, it was a marsupial, which means it kept its young in a pouch. Some people think *Diprotodon* looks a little like the koala. Perhaps, but only if you imagine the koala to be the size of a hippopotamus and fully capable of crunching a human skull between its two back molars! *Diprotodon* was a plant-eater – but hippos are also veggies and that hasn't stopped them killing people. So maybe the players should take a timeout and chill with an ice cream until their court is *Diprotodon*-free!

DIPROTODON
PRONOUNCED
Dye-PRO-toe-don

LIVED
Australia,
1.8 million–40,000 years
ago

LENGTH
Up to 4 m (13 ft)

WEIGHT
Up to 3 tonnes
(3.3 US tons)

REAR VIEW

Diprotodon's pouch faced backwards, so the baby's view of the world would have been framed by mum's hind legs! The modern Australian wombat also has a backwards-facing pouch. When it burrows, soil doesn't get in the pouch!

GIANT SLOTH
MEGATHERIUM

Today's sloths live in trees in South America and weigh 6 kg (13 lb) at most. That's less than a Jack Russell terrier. *Megatherium*, however, wouldn't last long in a tree, nor would the tree! It weighs 4 tonnes (4.4 US tons) – about the same as an elephant!

As you can see, this giant sloth can reach leaves in the treetops simply by standing on its hind legs. In this position, it is the same height as the tallest giraffe. And to get at any leaves still out of reach, it could use its large claws and powerful arms to pull branches down to its mouth. Scientists think *Megatherium* also had a long, strong tongue that it wrapped around the branches to strip off leaves and fresh growth. And if there were no trees to feed on? Then it would use its big claws to dig at plant roots. And there are lots in this garden to try!

MEGATHERIUM
PRONOUNCED
Meg-ah-THEE-ree-um
LIVED
South America,
2 million–10,000 years
ago
LENGTH
6 m (20 ft)
WEIGHT
4 tonnes (4.4 US tons)

KILLER CLAWS?

Megatherium's huge claws measured almost 30 cm (12 in) long and prevented it from putting its feet flat on the ground – it had to walk on the sides of its feet. Some scientists have even claimed that *Megatherium* used these claws to slash and kill other animals. They think it ate meat as well as plants.

CLIMB OR DIG?

Frenchman Georges Cuvier was the first to identify the giant sloth, in 1796. He thought its huge claws enabled it to climb trees. Then he changed his mind – probably when he realized it was too big to climb trees! He decided the sloth lived underground and used its claws to dig tunnels.

TOWERING CAMEL
TITANOTYLOPUS

There is only one winner in this camel race and it's the giant camel *Titanotylopus*. Just look at those legs go. *Titanotylopus* is twice the height of today's camels and the legs alone are taller than the jockey. There are a few questions you have to ask about this race, though. For a start, how did the jockey get on *Titanotylopus*? A stepladder? And, more importantly, how will he manage to stay on? It looks like it's going to be a bumpy ride!

Titanotylopus remains have been found across the American West – including Texas, Kansas and Arizona. But giant camel fossils have also been found in the Arctic! Yes, that's right – about 3.4 million years ago, camels lived on Ellesmere Island in Canada, opposite Greenland, one of the world's coldest, bleakest spots. This camel – known as the High Arctic camel – wasn't as big as *Titanotylopus* but it was still bigger by a third than today's camels.

TITANOTYLOPUS
PRONOUNCED
Tie-tan-oh-TIE-low-puss
LIVED
Plains of North America, Europe and Asia, 5 million–300,000 years ago
LENGTH
4 m (13 ft)
WEIGHT
1–2 tonnes
(1.1–2.2 US tons)

ARCTIC DRIFTER
The High Arctic camel was well-adapted for life in the cold. Its wide, flat feet enabled it to walk on snow, and as in the desert, it could live off energy stored in its hump.

KING OF THE GRASSLANDS

MAMMOTH

This is what we call a real stand-off: monster fire truck versus, er, monster. This is a Steppe mammoth, the largest mammoth that ever existed. It weighed twice as much as the largest elephant of today and its tusks were 5 m (16 ft) long.

You think this stand-off is just fantasy? Don't be so sure. In May 2013, on the island of Maly Lyakhovsky, north of Russia, a mammoth was found buried in the frozen ground. It had been eaten alive by wolves while stuck in a peat bog. Despite this grisly attack, most of its body parts were intact – including three legs, most of its body, and even its trunk. Its blood had also frozen – and from this, scientists are hoping to get DNA to clone a new mammoth. So maybe, in the future, the world really will be like the movie *Jurassic Park* and stand-offs like this will be an everyday happening.

MAMMOTH

LIVED
Europe and Asia,
5 million years ago–
1,650 BCE

SHOULDER HEIGHT
Up to 4 m (13 ft)

WEIGHT
10–15 tonnes
(11–16.5 US tons)

FIRE RESCUE

DIAL 911

END OF AN ERA

Why did mammoths die out?
Some scientists think that when the
Ice Age ended, around 12,000 years
ago, mammoths lost their habitat,
as open grasslands and woodlands
were replaced by forests. Others
think the animals were hunted to
extinction by humans. Perhaps both
these factors, combined with rising
sea levels, brought about the end of
these majestic beasts.

TIMELINE

ESTEMMENOSUCHUS

Named after the Greek for 'crowned crocodile'

Estemmenosuchus belonged to the therapsid group of reptiles from which mammals evolved. Therapsids had different teeth: incisors at the front, stabbing canines, and grinding molars at the back.

PARACERATHERIUM

Named after the Greek for 'near the hornless beast'

Paraceratherium, first discovered in 1907–08, was so-called because it resembled *Aceratherium*, another rhino-like creature, whose name means – yes, you guessed it – 'hornless beast'.

STUPENDEMYS

Named after the Greek for 'astonishing turle'

The earliest turtle evolved around 220 million years ago. When the dinosaurs died out about 66 million years ago, turtles survived because they could live on very little for a long time.

MOSCHOPS

Named after the Greek for 'calf face'

Moschops was also a therapsid. It had a 10-cm-thick (4-in) skull bone, so that didn't leave much room for the brain.

GIGANTOPITHECUS

Named after the Greek for 'giant ape'

The first time that the existence of *Gigantopithecus* came to light was in 1935, when palaeontologist Ralph von Koenigswald found an extremely large fossilized molar tooth in an apothecary shop in Hong Kong! (The Chinese call old animal teeth 'dragons' teeth' and use them in traditional medicine.)

267 MILLION YEARS AGO

Around 230 million years ago: First dinosaurs evolve

66 million years ago: End of the dinosaurs

ELASMOTHERIUM

Named after the Greek for 'thin plate beast'

When fossils from this giant, one-horned beast were first discovered in Siberia, they were thought to belong to the mythical unicorn. Stories were told of its horn being so large it had to be transported by sledge. *Elasmotherium* is still informally known as the 'Siberian unicorn'.

MAMMOTH

Derived from 'mamant' meaning 'Earth-horn' in the Mansi language of Russia

Steppe mammoths lived on the plains of Europe and Asia. To fuel their huge bodies, they ground up large amounts of grasses with their broad teeth.

DIPROTODON

Named after the Greek for 'two forward teeth'

In 2009–12, scientists found 50 *Diprotodons* in Queensland, Australia. The animals may have become trapped while searching for water. Teeth from crocs and lizards at the site suggest they were eaten alive by these reptiles.

TITANOTYLOPUS

Named after the Greek for 'knobby foot'

Camels originated in North America about 40 million years ago. They reached Asia across the Bering Strait, which used to be dry land between Alaska and Russia. They eventually made it to the Middle East and North Africa.

MEGATHERIUM

Named after the Greek for 'great beast'

Megatherium tracks left on the ground – as well as its bones – have been fossilized. These prove that it walked on both two feet and all fours.

UNCOVERING THE PAST

Without the careful and dedicated work of palaeontologists (pronounced: pay-lee-on-tol-o-gist), we would know nothing about our prehistoric past. These scientists search for fossils, the remains of extinct animals, to identify and understand early life forms.

A body fossil is the actual part of an animal, such as teeth or bones, preserved in rock. Fossils of the same animal can, of course, be discovered in different places. The first fossils found of the largest land mammal, *Paraceratherium* (above and see page 12), were discovered in Balochistan, Pakistan, in 1907–08, by the British geologist Guy Ellcock Pilgrim. Others have since been found in Kazakhstan, China and Mongolia,

No matter how mighty the original animal was, fossils of its body parts can be very delicate, and need to be wrapped up carefully. When scientists tried to move the first fossils of *Paraceratherium*, many of them shattered. Remember there weren't nice roads and modern cars in those days – most of the transportation was done on camels!

CRYPTIDS

Paraceratherium was a genuine discovery. Cryptids, on the other hand, are animals that people claim to have seen, but for which there is no scientific proof of existence. For example, 'Big Foot' is a large, hairy ape supposed to live in the forests of northwest USA, similar to the Yeti of the Himalayan mountains. And, of course, there is the Loch Ness monster (artist's impression, right), first 'sighted' lurking in its Scottish loch in 1933. But a famous photograph of it, supposedly taken the following year, has been proved to be a fake. The monster's head and neck were out of the water and the ripples on the water are completely out of proportion to them!

Even so, some people do think 'Nessie' exists and is a plesiosaur: a giant long-necked sea reptile from the time of the dinosaurs. Others have even claimed it is a sauropod, a long-necked dinosaur. Although why a land-dwelling dinosaur is living in a loch is anyone's guess! Also, Loch Ness was formed about 10,000 years ago – and plesiosaurs and sauropods lived more than 66 million years ago!

Extinction

Until the 19th century, most people did not think animals could go extinct. When a fossil of an unknown animal was found, experts thought it must live in an unexplored region of the world. Nowadays everyone knows that animals become extinct, and often because humans hunted them.

In North America, the sabre-toothed tiger and the mammoth went extinct at around the time humans arrived, 10,000 years ago. More recent extinctions include the elephant bird of Madagascar and the dodo (right), a flightless bird from the island of Mauritius. Both species died out around the 17th century. With the dodo, it was less than 100 years after the first humans settled on Mauritius.

INDEX

The Author

Matthew Rake lives in London, UK, and has worked in publishing for more than 20 years. He has written on a wide variety of topics for adults as well as children, including science, sport and the arts.

The Illustrator

Award-winning illustrator Simon Mendez combines his love of nature and drawing by working as an illustrator with a focus on scientific and natural subjects. He paints on a wide variety of themes but mainly concentrates on portraits and animal subjects. He lives in the United Kingdom.